Thanks to Steven Wille

First published in Belgium and Holland by Clavis Uitgeverij, Hasselt – Amsterdam, 2011
Copyright © 2011, Clavis Uitgeverij

English translation from the Dutch by Clavis Publishing Inc. New York
Copyright © 2015 for the English language edition: Clavis Publishing Inc. New York

Visit us on the web at www.clavisbooks.com

Astronauts and What They Do written and illustrated by Liesbet Slegers
Original title: *De astronaut*
Translated from the Dutch by Clavis Publishing

ISBN 978-1-60537-209-9

This book was printed in April 2015 at Proost Industries NV,
Everdongenlaan 23, 2300 Turnhout, Belgium

First Edition
10 9 8 7 6 5 4 3 2 1

Clavis Publishing supports the First Amendment and celebrates the right to read

Astronauts

and What They Do

Liesbet Slegers

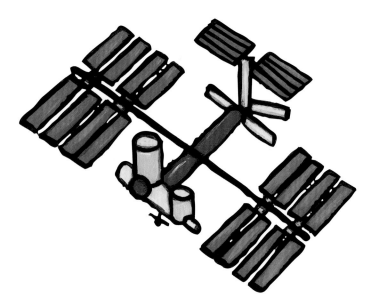

Clavis

NEW YORK

the earth

The earth is the planet on which all humans live.

We think the earth is very big, but in space

it is just a small ball, a little bigger than the moon.

At night when you can't see the sun, you can really see space.

It is black and quiet.

In space the sun, the moon, planets and stars float around.

Would you like to be able to fly into space?

cap

There are only a few people who are allowed to go into space.
An astronaut goes into space to see what can be found there.
To make the journey into space he needs a special space suit. Underneath his helmet the astronaut wears a little cap. The helmet, the special shoes and gloves are attached to the suit. This way the astronaut is completely protected. He needs to be protected because in space it can be terribly cold or awfully hot. Because there is no oxygen in space and humans need oxygen to breathe, there is a backpack with oxygen attached to the suit. On the belly of the space suit is a little computer. If something isn't working correctly, a little light on the computer starts to shine.

moon car

The astronaut goes into space in a space shuttle, which is a sort of rocket plane. In space there is no gravity so everything floats around – even the astronaut. His food and his toothbrush float too. How funny! That's why the astronaut sleeps in a sleeping bag that is attached to the wall. The astronaut uses the shuttle to travel to the space station that spins round the earth all the time. Several astronauts live and work in this special station. Everything they need in space, like their food, has to be brought from earth.

rocket

space shuttle

sleeping bag

space station

food in
little bags

Before the astronaut can go into space, he needs to practice long and hard. He learns how to float and how to prevent himself from getting sick when he somersaults too quickly.
The astronaut exercises a lot and eats a healthy diet. And of course he has to learn how to work with all the equipment in the space shuttle and the space station. That is awfully difficult!

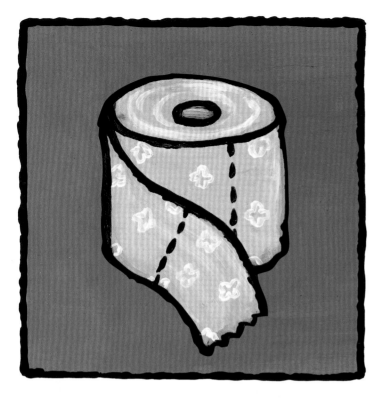

At last, it's time for lift off!

Before he puts on his space suit, an astronaut

goes to the toilet, because in the space shuttle

there is no regular bathroom.

It's hard work to put on a space suit!

There are many layers.

The astronauts are ready in their space shuttle.

They have buckled up tightly.

They have checked to make sure that everything is

in order: the engines, the fuel, the computers.

If just one thing doesn't work correctly, it can be disastrous.

Luckily the astronauts practiced well

and know what to do if something goes wrong.

The space shuttle is attached to rocket boosters.

Those make sure the shuttle will go into the air superfast.

It's time! The engines start. 3 – 2 – 1 – GO!

Very soon the space shuttle is high above the clouds. Wow!

First the astronauts fly through the earth's atmosphere and then

they arrive in space. When the rocket boosters are no longer

needed to move the shuttle forward, they are discarded.

That way the space shuttle flies to the space station alone.

The space shuttle heads for the space station that spins
around the earth all the time. When it gets there,
the shuttle connects to the station. There are other
astronauts already working in the space station.
Look, everything floats around!
Luckily the astronauts practiced how to move in zero gravity.

It's time to work on the special computers.

That way the astronaut can discover new things about space

and about nature. When he finds something interesting,

he passes it on to researchers on earth.

Sometimes the astronaut studies himself!

For example, is he hungrier in space or on earth?

Does he sweat more in space?

Those are interesting things to know.

If something has to be fixed outside of the space station
the astronaut has to go on a space walk. He puts on his
special suit, with the backpack that contains air
so he can breathe while he makes the space walk.
In space it is cold and quiet and very beautiful.
The astronaut has to be safely connected to the station.
If he weren't, he would float away into space.

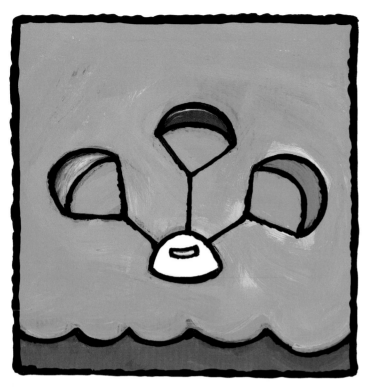

return with
the top of a rocket

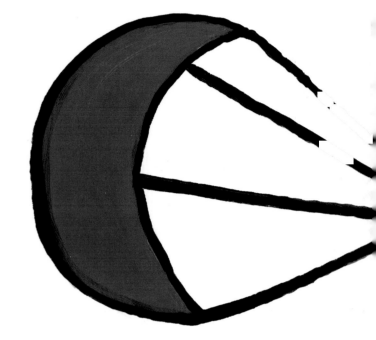

After a while the astronauts are done with their tests.

They leave the space station and go back into the space shuttle.

Then they return to earth.

Because a space shuttle lands at such a high speed,

the astronauts use a parachute to slow it down and help it stop.

Astronauts who use rockets to help them return to earth

may need as many as three parachutes to slow them down.

The tops of the rockets land on water.

Thanks to astronauts we now know more about space.

But there is still so much more to discover!

Space is so unbelievably big, and there is so much
that we don't know yet.

Maybe you will become an astronaut and adventure
among distant stars and planets.

Who knows, you could walk on the moon
or even discover a new planet!